ROMEO AND JULIET

ROMEO
AND JULIET

By William Shakespeare

Adapted by Diana Stewart
Illustrated by Charles Shaw

Raintree Publishers • Milwaukee • Toronto • Melbourne • London

INTRODUCTION

William Shakespeare was an actor. He wrote his plays to be performed by the acting company which he partly owned and managed. His plays were written to be performed, not read. It helps to understand how his plays work if the reader can imagine the stage they were acted on. Sometimes they were presented in large halls with a raised platform at one end. Sometimes they were performed in courtyards. But the stage he used most was a raised platform with the audience sitting and standing on three sides. The fourth wall had different levels so that the actors could be seen up above. Such a place was probably used for Juliet's window when she speaks to Romeo in the orchard below. At the back of the stage was probably a small place that could be closed off with curtains. This would be used for the tomb.

In Shakespeare's time very little scenery was used. A throne or a rock would be used to show a palace or a countryside. This made it possible for the many scenes to move very quickly. At the end of one scene the actors would leave and the new characters would come on immediately and begin the next scene. Audiences used their imagination to picture the scene, just as the reader has to when he or she reads the play.

Library of Congress Number: 79-24465

  3 4 5 6 7 8 9 0 84 83 82

Printed in the United States of America.

Library of Congress Cataloging in Publication Data

Stewart, Diana.
   Romeo and Juliet.

   SUMMARY: Presents a simplified text of the Shakespeare play in which two lovers are destroyed by the hatred of their families for one another.
   [1. Shakespeare, William, 1564-1616 — Adaptations]
I. Shakespeare, William, 1564-1616. Romeo and Juliet.
II. Shaw, Charles, 1941-   III. Title.
PR2878.R6S75   79-24465
ISBN 0-8172-1653-7 lib. bdg.

CAST OF CHARACTERS

Romeo, son of Montague

Juliet, daughter of Capulet

Nurse to Juliet

Friar Lawrence

Lord Capulet

Lady Capulet

Lord Montague

Lady Montague

Tybalt, nephew to Lady Capulet

Mercutio, a friend of Romeo

Benvolio, a friend of Romeo

Paris, a young count and suitor to Juliet's hand

The Prince of Verona

An Apothecary

A watchman of the city of Verona

Servants to Capulets and Montagues

Citizens of Verona

ACT I

Scene 1

The scene is a public road in Verona, Italy, in the sixteenth century. Servants from the House of Capulet and the House of Montague have met on the street and started a fight. Benvolio, a cousin of Romeo Montague, enters. He draws his sword to stop the fighting.

BENVOLIO. Stop, fools! Put up your swords. You don't know what you are doing!

(*Tybalt enters and draws his sword. He is a cousin of Juliet Capulet.*)

TYBALT. Turn, Benvolio; look upon thy death.

BENVOLIO. I only keep the peace. Put up thy sword.

TYBALT. What, sword drawn and talk of peace? I hate the word peace as I hate hell, all Montagues, and thee. Fight, coward!

(*Benvolio has no choice but to fight Tybalt. A crowd gathers, including Lord and Lady Capulet and Lord and Lady Montague. As the fighting gets more violent, the Prince of Verona enters with his followers. He is furious with both the noble families.*)

PRINCE. Stop, you enemies to peace!
On pain of torture, throw your weapons to the ground
And hear the sentence of your Prince.
Three fights by the Capulets and Montagues
Have broken the quiet of our streets.
If ever you disturb our streets again,
Your lives shall pay.
You, Capulet, shall go along with me;

And Montague, come to me this afternoon.
On pain of death, all men depart.

(They all exit but Benvolio. He greets Romeo, Lord Montague's son, as he enters.)

BENVOLIO. Good morrow, cousin.

ROMEO. Is the day so young?

BENVOLIO. It is just nine.

ROMEO. Ay me! Sad hours seem long.

BENVOLIO. What sadness makes Romeo's hours long? In love?

ROMEO. Out—

BENVOLIO. Of love?

ROMEO. Out of her favor where I am in love.

BENVOLIO. Tell me, who is it that you love?

ROMEO. Cousin, I do love a woman. But she hath sworn to love no man.

BENVOLIO. Be ruled by me; learn to forget her.

ROMEO. O, teach me how I should forget to think!

BENVOLIO. Forget by letting thine eyes examine other beauties.

ROMEO. He that is struck with love cannot forget the treasure of his heart. Farewell. Thou canst not teach me to forget.

(They exit.)

Scene 2

A street in Verona. Lord Capulet enters with Count Paris—a young nobleman of Verona who wants to marry Lord Capulet's daughter Juliet.

PARIS. But now, my lord, what say you? Will you give me the fair Juliet for my wife?

CAPULET. My child hath not seen the end of fourteen years;
Let two more summers pass
Before we think her ripe to be a bride.
Woo her, gentle Paris, win her heart.
This night I hold a feast.
I have invited many a guest,
And you among them. Come, go with me.

(*Capulet calls his servant over and gives him a paper with the names of the guests to be invited to the party that evening.*

CAPULET. Go, sirrah, through fair Verona;
Find those persons whose names are written there.

(*Capulet exits with Paris. The servant looks at the paper, but he cannot read. He sees Benvolio and Romeo entering and goes to them for help. He gives Romeo the list of names and asks him to read it aloud.*)

ROMEO. (After having read the list) A fair assembly. Where should these guests come?

SERVANT. To our house.

ROMEO. Whose house?

SERVANT. My master's. My master is the great rich Capulet; and if you be not of the house of Montague, I pray come and drink a cup of wine tonight.

(*As the servant leaves, Benvolio has an idea. He and Romeo will go to the Capulet party. Then Romeo can compare his love with all the other beautiful girls. This should cure his lovesickness.*)

BENVOLIO. (To Romeo) At this same feast of Capulet's
Comes the fair Rosaline whom thou so loves;
Go tonight, and compare her face with some that I shall show.

ROMEO. I'll go along, no such sight to be shown,
    But to rejoice in the beauty of mine own.

(They exit.)

Scene 3

The setting is a room in the Capulet house. Juliet's mother is talking to the old nurse who has raised Juliet from a baby.

LADY CAPULET. Nurse, where is my daughter? Call her forth to me.

NURSE. What, Juliet!

JULIET. (Entering) How now? Who calls?

NURSE. Your mother.

JULIET. Madam, I am here. What is your wish?

LADY CAPULET. Tell me, daughter Juliet, what think you of marriage?

JULIET. It is an honor that I dream not of.

LADY CAPULET. Well, think of marriage now. The brave Paris seeks you for his love. What say you? Can you love the gentleman?

(They are interrupted by a servingman.)

SERVANT. Madam, the guests are come, supper served up. I beg you follow straight.

LADY CAPULET. We follow thee. Juliet, the Count Paris awaits you.

(They exit.)

Scene 4

The scene is a hall in Capulet's house. Present are Lord

and Lady Capulet, Juliet, Tybalt, and the guests dressed in costumes and masks. Music begins and the company dances. Romeo and Benvolio are there in disguise. Romeo is looking at the girls, trying to find his beloved Rosaline, when he sees Juliet. All thought of Rosaline goes out of his head.

ROMEO. (To a servant) What lady is that which doth grace
    the hand of yonder knight?

SERVANT. I know not, sir.

ROMEO. O, she teaches the torches to burn bright!
    Did my heart love till now?
    For I never saw true beauty till this night.

    (Tybalt is standing near with Lord Capulet. He recognizes
    Romeo's voice.)

TYBALT. This voice belongs to a Montague.
    (To a servant) Get me my sword, boy.
    Now, by the honor of my kin,
    To strike him dead I hold it not a sin.

CAPULET. Why, how now, cousin? Why do you storm so?

TYBALT. Uncle, this is a Montague, our foe.

CAPULET. Young Romeo is it?

TYBALT. 'Tis he, that villain Romeo.

CAPULET. Be merry, gentle cousin, let him alone.
    And, to say truth, Verona brags of him
    To be a good and well-mannered youth.
    Therefore be patient; take no notice of him.

TYBALT. I'll not endure him!

CAPULET. He shall be endured! Am I the master here, or you? Go to! Go to! You are too quick to anger.

    (Tybalt is furious that Romeo has come to the party unin-
    vited. Too angry to stay and enjoy the dance, he leaves.

Romeo continues to watch Juliet from across the room. Their eyes meet. Both of them are struck with love. Romeo makes his way to her side. Gladly she goes with him to dance in a quiet corner.)

ROMEO. (Touching Juliet's hand) If I profane with my
　　unworthy hand
　　This holy shrine, the fine is this:
　　My lips will ready stand
　　To smooth that rough touch with a tender kiss.

JULIET. Good pilgrim, you do blame your hand too much,
　　Which well-mannered devotion shows in this,
　　For saints have hands that pilgrims' hands do touch,
　　And palm to palm is the pilgrim's kiss.

ROMEO. O, then, dear saint, let lips do what hands do!
　　(They kiss.)

NURSE. Madam, your mother wants a word with you.

ROMEO. (To the nurse after Juliet has gone) Who is her
　　mother?

NURSE. Why, sir, her mother is the lady of the house.

ROMEO. Is she a Capulet? Oh dear heart!

　　*(The end of the party has arrived. Lord Capulet wishes his
　　guests good night. As they leave, Juliet calls her nurse to her
　　side and points out Romeo.)*

JULIET. Come here, nurse. Who is yond gentleman?

NURSE. His name is Romeo, and a Montague, the only son
　　of your great enemy.

J~　　. My only love! Monstrous love it is to me
　　.hat I must love an enemy.

NURSE. What is this? What is this?

JULIET. A rhyme I learnt from one I danced with.

NURSE. Come, let's away; the strangers all are gone.
　　(They exit.)

14

ACT II

Scene 1

The scene is the orchard at the back of Capulet's house. Romeo has climbed the orchard wall in the hope of getting one more look at his beloved Juliet. His hope is rewarded when Juliet appears at the window to her room.

ROMEO. But soft! What light through yonder window
　　breaks?
　　It is the East, and Juliet is the sun!
　　It is my lady! Oh, it is my love!
　　Oh, that she knew she were!
　　See how she leans her cheek upon her hand!
　　Oh, that I were a glove upon that hand,
　　That I might touch that cheek!

JULIET. Ay me!

(She is unhappy because Romeo is a Montague.)

ROMEO. She speaks!

JULIET. O Romeo, Romeo! Wherefore art thou Romeo?
　　Deny thy father and refuse thy name;
　　Or, if thou will not, be but sworn my love,
　　And I'll no longer be a Capulet.

ROMEO. (To himself) Shall I hear more, or shall I speak
　　at this?

JULIET. 'Tis but thy name that is my enemy.
　　Thou art thyself, even though a Montague.
　　What's in a name? That which we call a rose
　　By any other name would smell as sweet.
　　Romeo, throw off thy name,
　　And for thy name, take all myself.

ROMEO. I take thee at thy word.
Call me but love, and I'll be new named;
Henceforth I never will be Romeo.

JULIET. What man art thou, thus hidden in the night?

ROMEO. By a name
I know not how to tell thee who I am.
My name, dear love, is hateful to myself
Because it is an enemy to thee.

JULIET. Art thou not Romeo, and a Montague?

ROMEO. Neither, fair maid, if either thee dislike.

JULIET. How camest thou hither, tell me, and why?
The orchard walls are high and hard to climb,
And the place death, considering who thou art,
If any of my kinsmen find thee here.

ROMEO. Alack, there lies more danger in thine eyes
Than twenty of their swords! Look but sweet,
And I am protected from their anger.

JULIET. By whose directions foundest thou this place?

ROMEO. By love.

JULIET. O gentle Romeo,
If thou dost love, say it faithfully.

ROMEO. What shall I swear by?

JULIET. Do not swear at all. Although I joy in thee,
I have no joy of this love tonight.
It is too rash, too sudden.
Good night, good night! As sweet rest
Come to thy heart as that within my breast!

ROMEO. O, will thou leave me so unsatisfied?

JULIET. What satisfaction canst thou have tonight?

ROMEO. The exchange of thy love's faithful vow for mine.

JULIET. If that thy aim of love be honorable,
Thy purpose marriage, send me word tomorrow,
And all my fortunes at thy foot I'll lay
And follow thee my lord throughout the world.

ROMEO. My sweet!

JULIET. Good night, good night! Parting is such sweet
sorrow
That I shall say good night till it be morrow.

Scene 2

The scene is Friar Lawrence's cell. The Friar is Romeo's old friend and teacher. Romeo has told the Friar of his love for Juliet, and the holy man has agreed to marry them. He hopes that this will end once and for all the feud between the two families. Romeo has sent word to Juliet through her nurse for her to meet him at the Friar's cell. Friar Lawrence and Romeo enter.

FRIAR. So smile the heavens upon this marriage
That afterward with sorrow chide us not!

ROMEO. Amen, amen! But come what sorrow,
It cannot equal the joy
That one short minute gives me in her sight.

(Enter Juliet.)

FRIAR. Here comes the lady.

JULIET. Good-day to you, father.

FRIAR. Romeo shall thank thee, daughter, for us both.
Come, come with me, for by your leaves,
You shall not stay alone till Holy Church make two
in one.

(They exit.)

ACT III

Scene 1

The scene is a public street in Verona, later in the day of Romeo and Juliet's wedding. Romeo enters from one side with Benvolio and Mercutio, his friends. From the other side come Tybalt and his friends.

BENVOLIO. By my head, here come the Capulets.

MERCUTIO. By my heel, I care not.

TYBALT. Gentlemen, good-day. A word with you.
    Romeo, the love I bear thee can afford
    No better term than this: thou art a villain.

(Romeo does not want to quarrel with Tybalt because he is Juliet's cousin. He tries to walk past him.)

ROMEO. Tybalt, villain am I none.
    Therefore farewell. I see thou knowest me not.

TYBALT. Boy, this shall not excuse the injuries
    That thou has done me; therefore turn and draw.

ROMEO. I do protest I never injured thee,
    And so, good Capulet—which name I value
    As dearly as mine own—be satisfied.

MERCUTIO. (Angry that Romeo is taking such insults from
    Tybalt)
    Tybalt, you ratcatcher!

TYBALT. What wouldst thou have with me?

MERCUTIO. Good King of Cats, nothing but one of your
    nine lives.

21

(Tybalt and Mercutio draw their swords and begin to fight.)

ROMEO. Gentle Mercutio, put thy sword up.
    Draw, Benvolio; beat down their weapons.
    Gentlemen, for shame! Stop this outrage!
    Tybalt, Mercutio, the Prince hath
    Forbid this fighting in Verona streets.
    Stop, Tybalt! Good Mercutio!

(Romeo tries to stop the fight. He comes between the two men, but he only gets in Mercutio's way. Tybalt sees an opening and thrusts his sword under Romeo's arm and into Mercutio. As Mercutio falls, Tybalt turns and runs.)

MERCUTIO. I am hurt.

BENVOLIO. What, art thou hurt?

MERCUTIO. Ay, ay, a scratch, a scratch.

ROMEO. Courage, man. The hurt cannot be much.

MERCUTIO. No, 'tis not so deep as a well, nor so wide as a church door; but 'tis enough, it will serve. A plague on both your houses! Zounds, a dog, a rat, a mouse, a cat, to scratch a man to death! Why the devil came you between us, Romeo? I was hurt under your arm.

ROMEO. I thought all for the best.

MERCUTIO. Help me into some house, Benvolio,
    Or I shall faint. A plague on both your houses!

(Benvolio helps Mercutio to exit. Romeo is left to curse himself for a coward.)

ROMEO. My friend hath got this mortal hurt
    In my behalf—my reputation stained
    With Tybalt's slander—Tybalt, that an hour
    Hath been my cousin. O sweet Juliet,
    Thy beauty hath made me weak!

(Benvolio returns from the house.)

BENVOLIO. O Romeo, Romeo, brave Mercutio is dead! And
here comes the furious Tybalt back again.

ROMEO. Tybalt alive in victory, and Mercutio dead?

(Tybalt enters.)

ROMEO. Now, Tybalt, take the "villain" back again
That late thou gavest me; for Mercutio's soul
Is but a little way above our heads,
Waiting for thine to keep him company.
Either thou or I, or both, must go with him.

*(The two men draw and fight. Romeo runs Tybalt through
with his sword, and Tybalt falls dead.)*

BENVOLIO. Romeo, away, be gone!
The citizens are up, and Tybalt slain.
The Prince will doom thee to death
If thou art taken. Quick, be gone, away!

*(Romeo runs off and the Prince enters with the Capulets and
the Montagues and townspeople.)*

PRINCE. Benvolio, who began this bloody fight?

BENVOLIO. Tybalt, here dead, whom Romeo's hand did kill
After Tybalt hit the life of stout Mercutio.

LADY CAPULET. He is a kinsman to the Montagues;
His loyalty makes him false, he speaks not true.
Tybalt, my cousin! O my brother's child!
Prince, I beg for justice, which thou must give.
Romeo slew Tybalt; Romeo must not live.

PRINCE. Tybalt slew Mercutio; Romeo slew him.
And for that offense
Immediately we do exile him hence.
Let Romeo leave in haste,
Else, when he is found, that hour is his last.

(They all exit.)

Scene 2

The scene is the Capulet orchard. Juliet is waiting there for word from Romeo when he will come. The nurse—the lovers' messenger—arrives in tears.

NURSE. Ah, alas! He's dead, he's dead, he's dead!
    We are undone, lady, we are undone!
    Alack the day! He's gone, he's killed, he's dead!
    O Romeo, Romeo!
    Who ever would have thought it? Romeo!

JULIET. What devil art thou that dost torment me thus?
    Hath Romeo slain himself?

NURSE. I saw the wound, I saw it with mine eyes,
    Here on his manly breast.
    A corpse, a bloody terrible corpse;
    Pale, pale as ashes, all covered in blood,
    I fainted at the sight.

JULIET. O, break, my heart! Break at once!

NURSE. O Tybalt, Tybalt, the best friend I had!
    O Tybalt! Honest gentleman!
    That I should live to see thee dead!

JULIET. Is Romeo killed and is Tybalt dead?
    My dearest cousin, and my dearer lord?

NURSE. Tybalt is gone, and Romeo banished;
    Romeo that killed him, he is banished.

JULIET. O God! Did Romeo's hand kill Tybalt?

NURSE. It did, it did! Alas the day, it did!
    Shame come to Romeo!

JULIET. Cursed be thy tongue
    For such a wish! He was not born to shame.
    Upon his brow shame is ashamed to sit.

NURSE. Will you speak well of him that killed your cousin?

JULIET. Shall I speak ill of him that is my husband?
    My husband lives, that Tybalt would have killed;
    And Tybalt is dead, that would have killed my
        husband.
    "Tybalt is dead, and Romeo—banished."
    Romeo is banished—to speak that word
    Is father, mother, Tybalt, Romeo, Juliet,
    All killed, all dead. "Romeo is banished"—
    In that word is death!
    Where is my father and my mother, nurse?

NURSE. Weeping and wailing over Tybalt's corpse.
    Will you go to them?

JULIET. They wash his wounds with tears. My tears shall
        fall
    When theirs are dry—for Romeo's banishment!

NURSE. Get to your chamber. I'll find Romeo
    To comfort you. I know well where he is.
    Your Romeo will be here tonight.
    I'll go to him; he is hid at Lawrence's cell.

JULIET. O, find him! Give this ring to my true knight
    And ask him come to take his last farewell.

    (They exit.)

Scene 3

The scene is Friar Lawrence's cell. Romeo is waiting for
the Friar to return with news of the Prince's judgment. The
Friar enters.

FRIAR. Romeo, come forth; come forth man.

ROMEO. Father, what news?

FRIAR. I bring thee news of the Prince's doom.
    Not thy death, but thy banishment.

27

ROMEO. Ha, banishment? Be merciful, say "death;"
   There is no world outside Verona's walls,
   But pain, torture, hell itself.

FRIAR. But the kind Prince hath pushed aside the law,
   And turned that black word "death" to "banishment."
   This is dear mercy.

ROMEO. 'Tis torture, and not mercy. Heaven is here
   Where Juliet lives; and every cat and dog
   And little mouse, every unworthy thing,
   Live here in heaven and may look on her;
   But Romeo may not.

FRIAR. Thou foolish mad man, hear me speak.

ROMEO. O, thou will speak again of banishment. Talk
      no more!
   Were thou as young as I, Juliet thy love,
   An hour but married, Tybalt murdered,
   And like me banished,
   Then mightest thou speak, then mightest thou tear
      thy hair,
   And fall upon the ground, as I do now.

(The nurse knocks.)

FRIAR. Arise, someone knocks. Good Romeo, hide thyself!
   Who knocks so hard?

NURSE. Let me come in, and you shall know my errand. I
   come from Lady Juliet.

FRIAR. Welcome then.

NURSE. O holy Friar, tell me, where is my lady's lord?
   Where is Romeo?

FRIAR. There on the ground, made drunk with his own
   tears.

NURSE. Even so lies Juliet,
   Blubbering and weeping, weeping and blubbering.
   Stand up, stand up! Stand, and be a man.

For Juliet's sake, for her sake, rise and stand!

ROMEO. Nurse, speak thou of Juliet? How is it with her?
　　Doth not she think me a murderer?
　　Where is she? And how doth she? And what says she?

NURSE. O, she says nothing, sir, but weeps and weeps;
　　And now falls on her bed, and then starts up,
　　On Tybalt calls; and then on Romeo cries,
　　And then falls down again.

　　(The news makes Romeo so miserable that he tries to stab himself with a knife, but the nurse snatches it from him.)

FRIAR. Art thou a man? Thy form says thou art;
　　Thy tears are womanish, thy wild acts show
　　The unreasonable fury of a beast.
　　Stir thee, man! Thy Juliet is alive.
　　The law that threatened death becomes thy friend
　　And turns it to exile. Listen to me!
　　Go to thy love and comfort her.
　　Come morning, thou shalt leave for Mantua,
　　Where thou shalt live till we can find a time
　　To reveal your marriage and beg pardon of the Prince.
　　Go first, nurse. Tell thy lady to hurry all
　　The house to bed. Romeo is coming.

NURSE. (To Romeo) My lord, I'll tell my lady you will come.

ROMEO. Farewell.

　　(They exit.)

Scene 4

　　The scene is a room in Capulet's house. Lord and Lady Capulet enter with Count Paris.

CAPULET. Sir Paris, I think my daughter will be ruled
　　by me.
　　Wife, go to her before you go to bed;

Tell her of Paris's love. Thursday, tell her,
She shall be married to this noble earl.

PARIS. My lord, I wish that Thursday were tomorrow.

CAPULET. Thursday be it then.
Prepare her, wife, for this wedding day.
Farewell, my lord.

Scene 5

The scene is Juliet's bedchamber. Romeo and Juliet have had their wedding night together, but morning is not far away and Romeo must leave by way of the window. The nurse enters.

NURSE. Madam!

JULIET. Nurse?

NURSE. Your lady mother is coming to your chamber.

(The nurse leaves.)

JULIET. Then, window, let day in and let life out.

ROMEO. Farewell, farewell! One kiss, and I'll depart.

(They kiss, and Romeo leaves through the window as Lady Capulet enters.)

JULIET. It is my lady mother. Is she to bed so late or up so early?

LADY CAPULET. Why, how now, Juliet?

JULIET. Madam, I am not well.

LADY CAPULET. Evermore weeping for your cousin's death?
What, will thou wash him from his grave with tears?
Have done. Some grief shows much love;
But much grief shows some want of wit.
Now I'll tell thee joyful news, girl.

JULIET. What news, your ladyship?

LADY CAPULET. Why, my child, early next Thursday
      morning
   The brave, young, and noble gentleman,
   The Count Paris—at Saint Peter's Church—
   Shall make thee a joyful bride.

JULIET. Now by Saint Peter's Church, and Peter too,
   He shall not make me there a joyful bride!
   I wonder at this haste, that I must wed
   Before he that will be my husband comes to woo.
   I pray you tell my lord and father, madam,
   I will not marry yet!

LADY CAPULET. Here comes your father. Tell him so
      yourself
   And see how he will take the news.

   (Lord Capulet enters with the nurse.)

CAPULET. How now, wife? Have you told her our plan?

LADY CAPULET. Ay, sir; but she will have none of it!
   I would the fool were married to her grave!

CAPULET. How? Will she not? Doth she not give us thanks?
   Is she not proud? Doth she not count her blest,
   Unworthy as she is, that we have arranged
   So worthy a gentleman to be her groom?

JULIET. Good father, I beg you on my knees,
   Hear me with patience.

CAPULET. Hang thee, young baggage!
   I tell thee what—get thee to church on Thursday
   Or never after look me in the face.

NURSE. God in heaven bless her!
   You are to blame, my lord, to scold her so.

CAPULET. Peace, you mumbling fool! It makes me mad!
   To have her matched; and having now provided
   A gentleman of noble parents,
   Of good fortune, youthful, and nobly trained,
   And then to have the fool answer "I'll not wed. I
      cannot love;

31

I am too young, I pray you pardon me!"
Think, lady; I do not jest.
Thursday is near; I'll give you to Count Paris,
Or beg, starve, die in the streets,
By my soul, I'll never again call thee daughter.

(He exits)

JULIET. O sweet my mother, cast me not away!
Delay this marriage for a month, a week!

LADY CAPULET. Talk not to me, for I'll not speak a word.
Do as thou will, for I have done with thee!

(She exits.)

JULIET. O God! How shall this be stopped?
My husband is on earth; my marriage vows recorded
in heaven.
Nurse, go in; and tell my lady that having displeased
my father,
I have gone to Friar Lawrence to make confession.
I'll ask the Friar for his help.
If all else fails, myself have the power to die.

ACT IV

Scene 1

The scene is in Friar Lawrence's cell. Juliet has come to
him for help. He is the only one that can save her from
marriage to Paris.

FRIAR. O Juliet, I already know thy grief;
I hear thou must on Thursday be married to Count
Paris.

JULIET. Tell me, Friar, how I may prevent it.
    Speak quickly. I long to die if thou canst not help me.

    (She takes a dagger from her belt and threatens to kill herself.)

FRIAR. Stop, daughter. I do see a kind of hope.
    If thou hast the courage, I'll give thee a remedy.

JULIET. And I will do it without fear or doubt,
    To live a pure wife to my sweet love.

FRIAR. Go home, then. Be merry, and give consent
    To marry Paris. Wednesday is tomorrow.
    Take thou this vial. When thou art in bed,
    Drink off its contents.
    When it runs through all thy veins,
    No warmth, no breath, shall show thou livest;
    The roses in thy lips and cheeks shall fade.
    Stiff and stark and cold, thou shalt appear like death
    For two and forty hours,
    And then awake as from a pleasant sleep.
    Now, when the bridegroom comes in the morning
    To awake thee from thy bed, there art thou dead.
    In thy best robes, uncovered,
    Thou shalt be laid in that ancient vault
    Where all the Capulets lie.
    In the meantime, before thou shalt awake,
    I shall write Romeo of our plan,
    And here shall he come; and he and I
    Will watch thy waking, and that very night
    Shall Romeo bear thee away to Mantua.
    And this shall free thee from thy shame.

    (Juliet reaches out and takes the vial filled with the drug.)

JULIET. Give me, give me! O, I am not afraid!
    Love gives me strength.
    Farewell, dear father.

35

Scene 2

The scene is Juliet's bedchamber. Night has come. She has told her father and mother that she will marry Paris in the morning. Nurse and Lady Capulet have helped her choose the clothes for her wedding and have now left her alone to sleep.

JULIET. (To her mother and the nurse as they leave)
Farewell!
(To herself) God knows when we shall meet again.
A faint cold fear thrills through my veins
That almost freezes up the heat of life.
Come, vial.

(*She holds the drug in her hands, but she is frightened.*)

What if this mixture does not work at all?
Shall I be married then tomorrow morning?

(*She grows more and more frightened of taking the drug.*)

What if it be a poison which the friar
Hath given me to have me dead,
Lest he should be blamed
Because he married me before to Romeo?
How if, when I am laid into the tomb,
I wake before the time that Romeo comes
And there die strangled? There's a fearful point!
Or if I wake, shall I not be driven mad?

(*As her mind imagines all the terrors of the tomb, she thinks Tybalt's ghost has come to haunt her.*)

O, look! I think I see my cousin's ghost
Seeking out Romeo. Stop, Tybalt, stop!
Romeo, Romeo, Romeo, I drink to thee!

(*She raises up the vial and drinks the drug and then falls upon her bed as though she is dead.*)

Scene 3

The scene is Juliet's chamber the next morning. All the preparations have been made for the wedding. Nurse enters to get Juliet ready for the marriage to Paris.

NURSE. Mistress! What, mistress! Juliet!
What, dressed, and in your clothes, and asleep again?
I must wake you. Lady! Lady! Lady!

(Nurse shakes her and tries to wake her, but the drug has done its work and Juliet seems to be dead.)

Alas, alas! Help! My lady's dead!

(Lady Capulet enters.)

LADY CAPULET. What noise is here? What is the matter?

NURSE. Look, look! O heavy day!

LADY CAPULET. O me, O me! My child, my life!
Help, help! Call help.

(Lord Capulet enters.)

CAPULET. For shame, bring Juliet forth; her lord is come.

LADY CAPULET. Alack the day, she's dead, she's dead, she's dead!

CAUPLET. Ha! Let me see her. Alas! She's cold,
And her joints are stiff;
Death lies on her like a frost
Upon the sweetest flower of all the field.

(The Friar enters with Count Paris.)

FRIAR. Come, is the bride ready to go to church?

CAPULET. Ready to go, but never to return.
O son, the night before thy wedding day
Hath Death been with thy wife. There she lies.

PARIS. Have I thought, love, to see this morning's face,
And doth it give me such a sight as this?

LADY CAPULET. Unhappy, hateful day!

NURSE. O woe! O woeful, woeful, woeful day!

CAPULET. O child, O child!
  Dead art thou—and with my child my joys are buried!

FRIAR. Dry up your tears, and in her best array
  Bear her to church.

CAPULET. All things we ordered for the marriage festival
  Turn now to black funeral. Our bridal flowers
  Serve for a buried corpse.

FRIAR. Sir, go you in; and madam, go with him:
  And go, Sir Paris. Everyone prepare
  To follow this fair corpse unto her grave.

ACT V

Scene 1

The scene is a street in Mantua. Romeo is there waiting for his messenger to return from Verona with word of Juliet. The servant arrives.

ROMEO. (To servant) News from Verona! How now,
  Dost thou bring me letters from the Friar?
  How doth my lady? Is my father well?
  How fares my Juliet?

SERVANT. Her body sleeps in Capulet's tomb,
  And her immortal soul lives with the angels.
  I saw her laid in her family's vault
  And came forth to tell you.
  O, pardon me for bringing this bad news, sir.

(Romeo is staggered by the news that Juliet is supposedly dead.)

ROMEO. Is it so? Then I defy you, stars!
Get me ink and paper and hire horses.
I will leave Mantua tonight. Get thee gone.

(The servant exits. Romeo stops to plan. If Juliet is dead, he no longer wants to go on living. Now he must decide on the way in which he will kill himself.)

ROMEO. Well, Juliet, I will lie with thee tonight.
Let's see for means. What, ho! Apothecary!

(The apothecary—a druggist—enters.)

APOTHECARY. Who calls so loud?

ROMEO. Come here, man. I see that thou art poor.
Here is forty ducats. Let me have
A dram of poison, such a fast-working poison
That the taker may fall dead.

(The apothecary takes out a vial of poison and gives it to Romeo.)

APOTHECARY. Put this in any liquid thing you will
And drink it off, and if you had the strength
Of twenty men, it would kill you straight.

ROMEO. (Handing him the money) There is thy gold.
Come, poison, go with me
To Juliet's grave; for there must I use thee.

Scene 2

The scene is the churchyard and the tomb belonging to the Capulets. Friar Lawrence has discovered that the letter he sent to Romeo to tell him of Juliet's pretended death did not reach him. He has also learned that Romeo is on his way to Verona. He hurries to the churchyard, but others are there before him. Count Paris has come to put flowers at Juliet's grave. Paris hears footsteps and hides as Romeo enters with his servant.

ROMEO. (To the servant) Take this letter. Early in the morning
    Deliver it to my lord and father. (Takes the torch from him)
    Give me the light. Upon thy life I tell thee,
    Do not try to stop me in my course.
    If thou dost, by heaven, I will tear thee joint by joint
    And throw thy limbs around this hungry churchyard.

SERVANT. I will be gone, sir, and not trouble ye.

(The servant leaves. Romeo opens the door to the tomb and is about to enter when Paris comes out of hiding.)

PARIS. This is the banished Montague
    That murdered my love's cousin.
    Stop, evil Montague! Obey,
    And go with me; for thou must die.

ROMEO. I must indeed; for death came I here.
    Good gentle youth, be gone and leave me.
    I beg thee, youth, put not another sin upon my head
    By moving me to anger. O, be gone!

PARIS. I do defy thee and take thee my prisoner.

ROMEO. Will thou enrage me? Then draw thy sword, boy!

(They both draw their swords and fight. Romeo runs Paris through. He falls.)

PARIS. O, I am killed! If thou be merciful,
    Open the tomb, and lay me with Juliet.

(He dies.)

ROMEO. Let me see this face.
    Mercutio's kinsman, noble Count Paris!
    What said my man as we rode? I think
    He told me Paris should have married Juliet.
    I'll bury him here by Juliet. Her beauty

Makes this tomb a place full of light.

(Romeo lays Paris's body in the tomb, then he turns to his beloved Juliet.)

ROMEO. O my love, my wife!
Death, that hath sucked the honey of thy breath,
Hath had no power yet upon thy beauty.
Eyes, look your last! Arms, take your last embrace!

(He takes a cup of poison in his hand.)

Here's to my love!

(He drinks it and kisses Juliet one last time.)

O true apothecary!
Thy drugs are quick. Thus with a kiss I die.

(He falls dead. Friar Lawrence comes into the churchyard and enters the tomb as Juliet begins to awaken.)

FRIAR. Romeo!
Alack, alack, what blood is this which stains
The entrance of the tomb?
Romeo! Who else? What, Paris too?
And covered in blood? The lady stirs.

JULIET. O Friar! Where is my lord?
I do remember well where I should be,
And there I am. Where is my Romeo?

FRIAR. I hear some noise. Lady, come from this nest
Of death. Come, come away.
Thy husband there lies dead; and Paris too.
Stay not to question, for the watchman is coming.
Come, go, good Juliet. I dare no longer stay.

JULIET. Go, get thee away, for I will not leave.

(The Friar leaves. Juliet goes to the dead Romeo.)

JULIET. What's here? A cup, closed in my true love's hand?
Poison, I see, hath brought his end.
O Romeo! Drunk all, and left no friendly drop

To help me after? I will kiss thy lips.
Perhaps some poison yet doth hang on them
To make me die.

(She kisses him.)

Thy lips are warm!

(She hears the noise of the watchmen coming. She takes Romeo's dagger and presses it to her breast.)

Yea, noise? Then I'll be quick. O happy dagger!
Rest here, and let me die. *(She stabs herself and falls.)*

(The watchmen see the open tomb and enter.)

CHIEF WATCHMAN. The ground is bloody.
Terrible sight! Here lies Count Paris dead;
And Juliet bleeding, warm, and newly dead.
Go tell the Prince; run to the Capulets;
Raise up the Montagues.

(A short time later the Prince enters with Lord and Lady Capulet, Lord Montague, and the Friar.)

PRINCE. Who calls us from our morning rest?

CHIEF WATCHMAN. Prince, here lies the Count Paris killed;
And Romeo dead; and Juliet, dead before,
Warm and new killed.

PRINCE. Search, seek, and find how this murder comes.
Friar, say at once what thou dost know of this.

FRIAR. I will be brief.
Romeo, there dead, was husband to that Juliet;
And she, there dead, that's Romeo's faithful wife.
I gave her a sleeping potion to keep her from a second
marriage.
Meantime I wrote to Romeo that he should come
hither.
But he which bore the letter was stopped by an
accident.
I came tonight to take her safely to my cell.

But when I came, some minutes before the time
Of her awakening, here lay the noble Paris and true
  Romeo dead.
She wakes; and I beg her to come forth with me;
But a noise did scare me from the tomb,
And she would not go with me,
But, it seems, did kill herself.
All this I know.

PRINCE. Where's Romeo's man? What can he say to this?

(Romeo's servant comes out from the shadows of the churchyard where he has been hiding.)

SERVANT. I brought my master news of Juliet's death;
And in haste he came from Mantua
To this same place, to this same tomb.
This letter he early asked me give his father.

(The Prince takes the letter from him and reads it.)

PRINCE. This letter doth make good the friar's words,
Their course of love, the news of her death;
And here he writes that he did buy poison
From a poor apothecary and with it
Came to this vault to die and lie with Juliet.
Where be these enemies? Capulet, Montague,
See the outcome of your hate.
All are punished.

(Both Lord Capulet and Lord Montague are stricken with grief. Their feud has caused the death of the people they love most. The feuding between the two families must end. Lord Capulet holds out his hand to Lord Montague in friendship.)

CAPULET. O brother Montague, give me thy hand.

MONTAGUE. Brother Capulet! *(The two shake hands.)*

PRINCE. A gloomy peace this morning with it brings.
The sun for sorrow will not show his head.
For never was a story of more woe
Than this of Juliet and her Romeo.

47

GLOSSARY

apothecary (ə päth′ ə ker′ ē) a person who sells drugs and medicines

baggage (bag′ ij) a worthless woman

banish (ban′ ish) to force someone to leave a place permanently

endure (in dur′) to put up with something patiently

kinsman (kinz′ mən) a member of the family

pilgrim (pil′ grəm) someone who travels to a holy place

plague (plāg) a bad disease that spreads quickly

profane (prō fān′) to treat something in an unholy way

thee, thou (thē, thaủ) an old word meaning "you"

thy (thī) an old word meaning "your"

vault (vȯlt) a room used for burial

vial (vī′ əl) a small container for holding liquids

villain (vīl′ ən) a person of low birth or class

DATE DUE

DATE DUE			

10/31/83

SIMPLY SCIENCE

Spring

by Darlene R. Stille

Content Advisers: Terrence E. Young Jr., M.Ed., M.L.S.,
Jefferson Parish (La.) Public Schools, and Janann Jenner, Ph.D.

Reading Adviser: Dr. Linda D. Labbo,
Department of Reading Education, College of Education,
The University of Georgia

 COMPASS POINT BOOKS
Minneapolis, Minnesota

Compass Point Books
3722 West 50th Street, #115
Minneapolis, MN 55410

Visit Compass Point Books on the Internet at *www.compasspointbooks.com* or e-mail your
request to *custserv@compasspointbooks.com*

Photographs ©:
Dave Schiefelbein, cover, 7; Photo Network/Margo Taussig Pinkerton, 4; Photo Network/B. Christensen, 5; Rob and Ann Simpson,
6, 28; Kent and Donna Dannen, 8; Mark A. Stack/Tom Stack and Associates, 11, 27; Photo Network/Gay Bumgarner, 12, 13;
Sharon Gerig/Tom Stack and Associates, 15; Richard Hamilton Smith, 16; Unicorn Stock Photos/Rod Furgason, 17; D. Cavagnaro/
Visuals Unlimited, 18; Leslie O'Shaaughnessy, 19; Jeff Greenberg/Visuals Unlimited, 20; Unicorn Stock Photos/Dede Gilman, 22;
Richard Demler, 23; Photo Network/Robert Grubbs, 24; James P. Rowan, 25; Merrilee Thomas/Tom Stack and Associates, 26;
Mark Gibson/Visuals Unlimited, 29.

Editors: E. Russell Primm, Emily J. Dolbear, and Melissa Stewart
Photo Researcher: Svetlana Zhurkina
Photo Selector: Matthew Eisentrager-Warner
Designer: Bradfordesign, Inc.

Library of Congress Cataloging-in-Publication Data

Stille, Darlene R.
   Spring / by Darlene Stille.
     p. cm. — (Simply science)
   Includes bibliographical references and index.
   ISBN 0-7565-0094-X (hardcover : lib. bdg.)
     1. Spring—Juvenile literature. [1. Spring.] I. Title. II. Simply science (Minneapolis, Minn.)
QB637.5 .S75 2001
508.2—dc21   00-011002

Table of Contents

Signs of Spring

Have you ever heard people say, "That's a sign of spring"? They had seen something that told them the cold days of winter were almost over.

A warm, sunny day could be a sign of spring. A robin could be a sign of spring too. A robin is a bird that **migrates**. It flies to warmer places in the winter and comes back in the spring. A tree with tiny buds on it is a sure sign that spring is on its way.

Pink cherry blossoms help show spring is coming.

When robins appear, winter is ready to end.

What Is Spring?

Spring is a season. There are four seasons in a year. The other seasons are summer, fall, and winter. Spring comes after winter and before summer.

Ask your friends if they can name the months of spring. That is a trick question. Spring comes at different times in different parts of the world. If you look at a **globe**, you will see that Earth is shaped like a big ball. Can you find a line running around the middle of the globe?

Visitors to Africa can stand on the imaginary equator line.

A barn near fields of wheat in springtime ▶

This line does not really exist. It is an imaginary line called the **equator**.

The equator divides Earth into two parts. The area above the equator is called the **Northern Hemisphere**. The area below the equator is called the **Southern Hemisphere**.

In the Northern Hemisphere, spring officially begins around March 21. It lasts until around June 21.

In the Southern Hemisphere, spring officially begins around September 21. It lasts until around December 21. When it is spring in the Northern Hemisphere, it is fall in the Southern Hemisphere.

◀ *Spring in the United States. It is in the Northern Hemisphere.*

Spring Brings Changes

In some places, spring is very different from winter. In other places, all four seasons are almost the same.

For example, there are no seasons at all at the equator. It is always hot there. Winter is warm in places close to the equator. Spring does not bring big changes in places where

Both winter and spring are warm in Florida.

Close to the equator, people can swim all year long.

winter is warm. Winter is cold in places far away from the equator. Spring brings big changes in places where winters are cold.

If you live in a place where winters are cold, you know that the grass turns brown in the fall. In the winter, it is covered with snow. In spring, the snow melts. Grass turns green again when the sun makes the days warmer.

◀ Winter and spring make the landscape look very different. ▶

Some trees have no leaves all winter long, but watch these trees when the weather gets warmer. Tiny buds appear on tree branches in spring. A few weeks later, the buds become leaves.

Many flowers bloom in the spring. The crocus is one of the first spring flowers. A crocus may even poke its head up through the snow. Daffodils and tulips are also spring flowers. They grow again every year.

Some flowers do not grow again every year. They grow from seeds that must be planted each spring.

A crocus bud peeking through the snow ▶

Spring Planting

In the Northern Hemisphere, spring begins at the end of March. That is the time when farmers and gardeners begin to plant seeds. First, they dig up the **soil**. Then they drop seeds in the ground and cover them with soil.

Farmers plant fields of crops. Some farmers plant wheat or corn. Other farmers plant

This farmer stands in his rows of corn plants.

Planting tulips in the ground ▶

vegetables. Many farmers use machines today to plant crops in rows. The plants grow all through the summer. In the fall, farmers **harvest** the crops, and we eat the crops as food.

Gardeners plant flowers. They may also plant carrots, cucumbers, and other vegetables. Gardens are much smaller than farm fields.

A gardener looking after her vegetables

You can watch plants grow from seeds indoors.

Plant Your Own Seeds

To see how plants grow, try planting some bean seeds. You will need a few bean seeds, some paper cups, a dinner plate or tray, some potting soil, and water.

Poke a few holes in the bottom of three or four paper cups. Place the cups on the plate or tray. Add potting soil to the cups until they are almost full. Push one seed into the soil in each

cup. The seeds should be about 1 inch (2.5 centimeters) below the top of the soil.

Place the plate or tray near a window where the sun shines in. Keep the soil wet.

Look at the cups every day. Write down what you see in a notebook. How long does it take for plants to spring out of the soil? When do the leaves appear? How tall do the plants grow? How are the plants in the cups and the plants outdoors the same? How are they different?

◀ *What do you learn from your plants?*

Springing into Action

Plants are not the only things that "wake up" in spring. Suddenly, there is life everywhere. Earthworms burrow through the soil. Caterpillars crawl on the new leaves. Flies, bees, and other insects zip through the air.

Look—and listen—for the birds. Do you see them flying or making nests? Do you

Hungry checkerspot butterfly caterpillars

Honey bees are a familiar sight in spring.

hear them singing? Some birds stay in cold places during the winter, but many birds migrate. They fly to warmer places in winter and come back in spring.

After two birds build a nest, the female bird lays eggs there. Soon baby birds hatch from the eggs. The mother or father bird brings food for the chicks. If the chicks are lucky, they will get a big worm for dinner.

The weather changes in spring. It gets warmer

A robin feeding a worm to her chicks

Canada geese are migrating birds.

and wetter. There may be many rainy days. You may not like that, but rain is good for plants. It helps grasses, trees, and flowers grow.

Sometimes spring rainstorms have thunder and lightning. These storms may also have powerful winds—or even **tornadoes**. Tornadoes are strong winds that blow in a circle. Small tornadoes can suck up dust and dirt. Big tornadoes can pick up cars and knock down houses.

Spring also brings dangerous tornadoes.

A spring thunderstorm ▶

Spring Turns into Summer

You can feel the days get warmer during spring. You can see that each spring day has more and more daylight. You can play outdoors a little later every day. In the Northern Hemisphere, the days are warm and long by the end of June. That is when spring ends and summer begins.

When spring ends, days are warmer and longer.

In spring, you can play ▶ outside longer.

Glossary

equator—an imaginary line around the center of Earth

globe—a round model of Earth that shows oceans and land

harvest—to gather crops

migrate—to travel to a warmer part of the world to find food or have young

Northern Hemisphere—the half of Earth that is above, or north of, the equator

soil—a mixture of broken-up rocks and rotting plant and animal material

Southern Hemisphere—the half of Earth that is below, or south of, the equator

tornadoes—small, spiraling storms with dangerous winds

Did You Know?

- Have you ever heard someone say, "April showers bring May flowers"? There is some truth to that old saying. April is often a rainy month, and many spring flowers bloom in May.

- Some parts of the world have just two seasons—the wet season and the dry season.

- Birds are not the only animals that migrate. Some fish, mammals, and insects migrate too.

Want to Know More?

At the Library

Ross, Kathy, and Vicky Enright (illustrator). *Crafts to Make in the Spring.* Brookfield, Conn.: Millbrook Press, 1999.

Sipiera, Paul P., and Diane M. Sipiera. *Seasons.* Danbury, Conn.: Children's Press, 1998.

Supraner, Robyn. *I Can Read about Seasons.* Mahwah, N.J.: Troll, 1999.

On the Web

Crafts for Kids

http://craftsforkids.about.com/parenting/craftsforkids

For dozens of craft projects related to the current season

Through the Mail

Farmers' Almanac Order Desk

P.O. Box 1609

Mount Hope Avenue

Lewiston, ME 04241

To order a seasonal guide with long-range weather forecasts

On the Road

The North Carolina Azalea Festival

P.O. Box 51

Wilmington, NC 28402

910/763-0905

To find out about attending this spring festival or to request a catalog about spring vegetables and flowers and their seeds

Index

About the Author

Darlene R. Stille is a science editor and writer. She has lived in Chicago, Illinois, all her life. When she was in high school, she fell in love with science. While attending the University of Illinois, she discovered that she also enjoyed writing. Today she feels fortunate to have a career that allows her to pursue both her interests. Darlene R. Stille has written more than thirty books for young people.